Poems That Rhyme All Of The Time

By
Paul Wilkins

Copyright © 2025 Paul Wilkins

ISBN: 978-1-917601-69-6

All rights reserved, including the right to reproduce this book, or portions thereof in any form. No part of this text may be reproduced, transmitted, downloaded, decompiled, reverse engineered, or stored, in any form or introduced into any information storage and retrieval system, in any form or by any means, whether electronic or mechanical without the express written permission of the author.

Introduction

Here is a collection of some of my favourite poems.

I hope you enjoy reading them as much as I enjoyed writing them.

They all humorously rhyme.

Paul Wilkins

Table of Contents

Love, Joy And Delight 8
Love And Joyfulness 9
Pirates 10
Waiter Me 11
40 Years Of Dad's Army 12
40th Anniversary Of Volunteers Week 13
50 Years Of 007 James Bond 14
50 Years Of Blue Peter 15
50 Years Of Coronation Street 16
50th Anniversary Of Moon Landing 17
75 Years Of The National Health Service (NHS) 18
80 Years Of Oxfam Charity 19
130 Years Of Blackpool Tower 20
200 Years Of The Royal National Lifeboat Institution (RNLI) . 21
200 Years Of The Royal Society For The Prevention Of Cruelty To Animals (RSPCA) 22
A Busy Sunshiny Day 23
A Friend Of Mine 24
A New Promising Friendship 25
A Super Poem about 'Superman' 26
A True Or Phoney Statement 27
AFC Fylde Charity 28
Angels 29
Astrological Horoscopes 30
At The Front Of Blackpool 31

Being Haunted By Ghosts 32
Betting On The Horse Races 33
Bugs Bunny 34
Bull's-Eye 35
Clever Hercule Poirot 36
Darkness 37
Disability Equality 38
European Champions 2022 The England Lionesses 39
Eye To Eye 40
Farming Away 41
Getting Up Early In The Morning, Occasionally Yawning 42
Going For A Pub Meal 43
Going To The Library 44
Healed With All The Power Of Love 45
In The British Army 46
In The Countryside 47
Magic Lost But Found 48
Pets And Owners To The Rescue 49
'Ping' Pong Merrily On High 50
Poetic Medicine 51
Sailing At Sea In The Royal Navy 52
Scouting and Abouting 53
Sharing A Heart 54
Sir William Shakespeare 55
Sir Winston Churchill 56
Smile And The World Smiles With You 57
Some Difficult Poetry 58

Someone To Have By My Side In The Countryside	59
Take A Break By Playing Snooker	60
The 1966 FIFA World Cup	62
The Best Of Preston City	63
The Cowboys	64
The Dangerous Fire Of Smoke	65
The Heroes Batman and Robin	66
The Life Of Dame Agatha Christie	67
The Life Of Martin Luther King	68
The Manchester United 2007/08 Double	69
The Royal Air Force (RAF)	70
The School Crossing Patrol Officers	71
The Staircase	72
The Temptation Of Chocolate	73
The World Hero Nelson Mandela	74
Together Keeping Afloat	75
Tom And Jerry	76
Treble Win In Season 1998/99	77
Ukraine Today	78
Vice-Admiral Horatio Nelson	79
What 'We' Did Together	80
William Wordsworth	81
Worldwide Climate Change	82

Love, Joy And Delight

1) Your mind and emotion hold the key
   They're the things to set you free
   What 'er the day
   What 'er the night
   Fulfil yourself with love, joy and delight

2) Sadness and worry
   Gets you nowhere at all
   Just up the wall
   What 'er the day
   What 'er the night
   Fulfil yourself with love, joy and delight

3) With faith in the Lord
   And determination
   You may live a long and happy life
   What 'er the day
   What 'er the night
   Fulfil yourself with love, joy and delight

4) Let people come first where 'er you go
   That's a thought
   All people should show
   What 'er the day
   What 'er the night
   Fulfil yourself with love, joy and delight

   Love, joy and delight
   Love, joy and delight

© Paul Wilkins 1993

Love And Joyfulness

1) Love holds the key
   Of setting you free
   Victory through it is found
   Emotionally all round

2) Joyfulness is very good
   Outstanding all that it could
   Yes, use it quite a lot you completely should

3) And amazement then comes your way
   Nothing leading you astray
   Developmental promises had each and every day

4) Delightfulness then comes about
   Entirely without a single doubt
   Laughter then totally had
   Intending to avoid you from at all feeling sad
   Gladness instead on it's way
   Hip hip hurray
   There's now all round triumphant happiness today

   © Paul Wilkins 14/06/2023

Pirates

1) Pirates used to sail along the seas
   Doing as they pleased
   They invaded many other ships for treasure
   And found counting what they'd gained a pleasure

2) The jolly roger was often hoisted in the daylight
   Which brought to many passing ships a fright
   Much theft took place
   Which was a large disgrace

3) On pirate ships the captives were killed quite frank
   Some were made to walk the plank
   At which the pirates enjoyed and laughed
   Though it was so horrible and daft

4) Pirates buried things on many far off islands
   What they'd had a cheek to thieve
   With the plan to return there one day
   To regain what they'd attacked ships to achieve

5) To these pirates, thank goodness, there finally came an end
   The trouble at sea to deeply descend
   When the Navy's tracking was found
   And the catching and avoiding of them bound

6) Today there still may be some treasure islands
   Of which no-one knows
   But to which someone someday goes
   And feel out of their mind
   With what they find

© Paul Wilkins 2000

Waiter Me

1) At quarter to eight
   My breakfast I ate
   Having a little debate
   Over whether to work I'd be late

2) I then opened my gate
   At half past eight
   Now for the bus I needed to wait
   Whilst in the cool wind that I hate

3) In the cafe I was told off for being late
   Then I needed to as usual wait
   Serve lots of people a big breakfast plate
   Though hoping they'd not put on too much weight

4) Then later in the cafe I saw a mate
   Who'd just turned 28
   And had with him his partner called Kate
   Who him being married to had been a big fate

© Paul Wilkins 28/01/2019

40 Years Of Dad's Army

1) The T.V. series 'Dad's Army' has been going for a while
   Bringing to many faces a sad memory, and smile
   Looking at brave people helping Britain during the world war
   Which they'd never at all done before
   Captain Mainwaring really got the supportive soldiers doing well
   As time did have to tell

2) With it starting in 1968 quite truly
   This is the 40th year of 'Dad's Army' being on T.V.
   In which the soldiers had many a mission to achieve
   Before Sergeant Wilson let them have some leave
   Captain Mainwaring really got the supportive soldiers doing well
   As time did have to tell

3) Lance Corporal Jones was often saying 'Don't Panic' to the rest
   Wanting them not to fail their many a big test
   Whilst miserable old Scotsman, Private Frazer, without delay
   Was always saying 'We're doomed!' each and every day
   Captain Mainwaring really got the supportive soldiers doing well
   As time did have to tell

4) Private Godfrey was always asking if he could 'be excused'
   Being in the troop he was not at all amused
   Private Pike was a bit of a 'Mummy's boy'
   With his Mother always with Sergeant Wilson having joy
   Captain Mainwaring really got the supportive soldiers doing well
   As time did have to tell

5) Private Walker to overcome his awkward war feelings
   Was always making a living by shady dealings
   Yes 'Dad's Army' have for years been up to a lot
   This series will be stopped being shown? 'Definitely Not'
   Captain Mainwaring really got the supportive soldiers doing well
   As time did have to tell

© Paul Wilkins 11/09/08

40th Anniversary Of Volunteers Week

1) It's Volunteers Week 2024 from the 3rd to 9th June yes
   To be marked with appreciation or so I guess
   Thanks to be given to lots of generous volunteers
   Who deserve joyful parties with no fears

2) It's 40 years of Volunteers Week in June 2024
   People helping out like never before
   Covering oh quite a long distance
   To many charities come of great big assistance

3) Together we'll now have to have a volunteer's celebration
   With not a slight bit of hesitation
   Them supporting the NHS and plenty a charity
   Largely valued by both you and me

4) We thank all the Volunteer Leaders too
   Who recruit and position quite a few
   And hopefully with continued support
   All Voluntary Work will go just like it ought

© Paul Wilkins 03/06/2024

50 Years Of 007 James Bond

1) Ian Fleming's Secret Agent 007 James Bond
   Has been going for 50 years
   Bringing lots and lots of cheers
   With both 'M' and 'Q's permission
   He's gone on many a different mission
   James Bond sorted 'Miss Moneypenny' out
   And did that without a doubt

2) Sean Connery in 'Dr No' was the first James Bond
   Of which many people were quite fond
   Then before much time was gone
   007 film-wise George Cazenby starred in one
   James Bond sorted 'Goldfinger' out
   And did that without a doubt

3) Roger Moore in 'Live and Let Die' became 007
   And in many other James Bond films
   Took stories from terror to heaven
   Timothy Dalton was then next to be on T.V.
   To be seen as 007 in lots of action by you and me
   James Bond sorted 'Jaws' out
   And did that without a doubt

4) Pierce Brosnan starred as James Bond too
   Had watching 'Tomorrow Never Dies' quite a few
   Then Daniel Craig as the Secret Agent took a place
   Who's going to be seen with many a new 007 film to face
   James Bond sorted 'Renard' out
   And did that without a doubt

5) In each film along with drinking some shaken not stirred 007 had a lot to do
   Vehicle and equipment-wise went through quite a few
   Although he had many an awkward task maybe
   He was always conclusively comforted by many a nice lady
   James Bond sorted 'The Man With The Golden Gun' out
   And did that without a doubt

© Paul Wilkins 17/01/2012

50 Years Of Blue Peter

1) 'Blue Peter' has now been going for 50 years
   Yes from 1958 to 2008 been bringing many young children cheers
   Valerie Singleton hosted it in 1962-72
   Bringing lots of entertainment for me and you

2) In 1965-78 John Noakes and his nice dog took part
   Into children's activities putting their heart
   With Peter Purves helping out too
   On children's T.V. attracting quite a few

3) In the 1970's and 80's Simon Groom, Peter Duncan and Janet Ellis
   Were on children's T.V.
   Giving many creative and amusement ideas to you and me
   Before in the 1990's 'Blue Peter' was run by Tim Vincent and Anthea Turner
   Making many a child become a very clever learner

4) With help from Konnie Huq and many more
   This programme's still going like many times before
   And I'm sure 'Blue Peter' will be watched for a very long while
   Continuing to bring many children a smile

© Paul Wilkins 20/09/08

50 Years Of Coronation Street

1) Coronation Street's now been going 50 years
   Which brings lots and lots of cheers
   Everyone's been watching it for ages
   Going through many different stages

2) In 1960 Tony Warren first got it going on T.V.
   With Ken Barlow one of the first for us to see
   It was in black and white until 1969
   When in colour it looked even more fine

3) The programme's theme tune for us all to very often hear
   Was put together by someone called Eric Spear
   It's really been going for a long spell
   With lots of different characters and tales to tell

4) It's had some of the biggest audiences of ever
   In 1981 when Ken Barlow and Deidre Longton got together
   And in December 1987 when Hilda Ogden left the show
   At which she'd had a very good cleaner's go

5) Through Coronation Street we've had many a story to learn
   Many of them including things happening at the Rovers Return
   And we all hope that it continues to do well
   Both now and in what the future has to tell

© Paul Wilkins 09/12/2010

50th Anniversary Of Moon Landing

1) With everything going quite fine
   The US Apollo 11 had a blast-off on the 16th July 1969
   And to be deeply applaud
   Neil Armstrong, Buzz Aldrin and Michael Collins boldly were based on board

2) With millions of people on the planet earth drinking to it with wine
   The Apollo lunar landed on the Moon on the 20th July 1969
   Which with no hesitation
   Was to make way for lots of future space exploration

3) Armstrong said 'Houston, Tranquillity Base here, The Eagle has landed'
   Then to have the pleasure of first step on the Moon he was handed
   Followed by both his colleagues yes
   Who as astronauts were very proud to do so or so I guess

4) These three astronauts just after landing on the Moon
   Hosting a US flag on it were on Worldwide TV to be seen soon
   Followed by lots and lots of celebration
   With people showing this achievement plenty of appreciation

5) In July 2019 Cities globally have held events to celebrate the 50th anniversary of this
   And put together many activities not to miss
   With still living Buzz Aldrin and Michael Collins appearing on TV
   To along with unfortunately dead Neil Armstrong be very proud of by you and me

© Paul Wilkins 20/07/2019

75 Years Of The National Health Service (NHS)

1) To be given lots of thankfulness and tears
   Now the NHS has been going for 75 years
   First founded in the year 1948
   Following the Windrush successful ethnic debate
   For the NHS Ambulance to get to you on time
   Just carefully dial the number 111 or 999

2) Wanting to lots of health problems come of assistance
   The NHS has covered oh quite a distance
   Recently with COVID-19 research and development they helped everyone out
   And did that very well without a doubt
   For the NHS Ambulance to get to you on time
   Just carefully dial the number 111 or 999

3) With the Consultant and Surgeon's co-operation
   The NHS has carried out many a life saving operation
   Helping people out mentally and physically yes
   And for a quite generous cheap price or so I guess
   For the NHS Ambulance to get to you on time
   Just carefully dial the number 111 or 999

4) We owe all the NHS staff, including Ambulance Paramedics and volunteers, a big thank-you
   Quite regularly saving the lives of me and you
   The GP's, Psychologists, Psychiatrists, Consultants, Surgeons and Nurses to be seen everywhere
   Showing to us all a real lot of care
   For the NHS Ambulance to get to you on time
   Just carefully dial the number 111 or 999

5) Now with the NHS Charity Association
   We'll all need to give a good occasional donation
   Hoping all goes extremely well
   In what the future of the all round NHS has to tell
   For the NHS Ambulance to get to you on time
   Just carefully dial the number 111 or 999

© Paul Wilkins 05/07/2023

80 Years Of Oxfam Charity

1) Oxfam Charity has now been going for 80 years' time
   With commitments to supporting anti-racism, feminism and shifting power going quite fine
   And it's covered a very big distance
   To in these areas, Worldwide, come of assistance

2) Demonstrating for the public what it's meant
   Oxfam has organized many a fund-raising event
   Had lots of staff and volunteers helping out
   Showing lots of generous support, no doubt

3) Thanks to plenty a warm heart
   In ending poverty Oxfam has played a part
   Largely with Charity shops I guess
   Which appreciates regular donations definitely yes

4) Charities like Oxfam will hopefully continue going for ages
   Helping out, all those in need, through different stages
   And with no hesitation
   At all its successful anniversaries have a good celebration

© Paul Wilkins 02/10/2022

130 Years Of Blackpool Tower

1) To become a world-wide known attraction never seen before
   Blackpool Tower was opened to the public on the 14th May 1894
   So to everyone with celebration to be told
   It has now, this year, reached 130 years old

2) Being able to have a very large view
   Blackpool Tower is visited each year by quite a few
   Around 1 million people going up it each year yes
   Though they all need some guts for the height or so I guess

3) With not a slight bit of hesitation
   Blackpool Tower often has on show many an illumination
   Shining out brightly late at night
   To all the passer-by's deep delight

4) Blackpool Tower as well as bring a fantastic sight
   Has a famous Town Ballroom, and Tower Circus to everyone's delight
   With entirely everything going fine
   It provides great entertainment all of the time

© Paul Wilkins 14/05/2024

200 Years Of The Royal National Lifeboat Institution (RNLI)

1) Sir William Hillary set up plans for a national lifeboat service on the 4th March 1824
   Which, with the MP Thomas Wilson's approval, got more life saving than ever before
   Later this was to be called the RNLI
   That has now been successfully going for 200 years no lie

2) The RNLI Headquarters is in Poole, Dorset UK yes
   Though it has 238 lifeboat stations operating on more than 200 beaches or so I guess
   Covering the UK, Ireland, Channel Islands and Isle of Man
   Doing for those stranded at sea totally all that they can

3) The RNLI is funded mainly by legacies and many a donation
   To, out at sea, save plenty a life with no hesitation
   Relying on unpaid volunteer after volunteer
   Who are all very brave and a hero year after year

4) So to the RNLI we owe a big thank-you
   For rescuing, at sea, oh quite a few
   And to manage doing everything that it ought
   Hope this charity continues to get all the needed generous support

© Paul Wilkins 04/03/2024

200 Years Of The Royal Society For The Prevention Of Cruelty To Animals (RSPCA)

1) It's the 200th anniversary of the England and Wales RSPCA today
   Who have come to the rescue of many an animal with no delay
   To provide assistance never seen before
   This charity was first founded on the 16th June 1824

2) This is the oldest and largest animal welfare organisation in the world yes
   Though lots of others have been formed worldwide or so I guess
   Completely helping plenty a different animal out
   By deeply assisting them in staying well no doubt

3) Over the last 200 years for creature after creature
   There has, through mankind, been provided plenty a life-saving feature
   Worldwide people covering oh quite a distance
   To animal's health and safety come of much great assistance

4) Today there will be lots of RSPCA celebration
   With not a slight bit of hesitation
   Hoping it's generous support will continue forever
   Animal creatures neglected again at all never

© Paul Wilkins 16/06/2024

A Busy Sunshiny Day

1) Some farmers get worn off their feet
   Hanging out many a sheet
   In the garden alongside the wheat
   Whilst putting up with the heat

1) They then feeling no defeat
   Manage to recover from plenty a feat
   And have something to eat
   As watching the TV Quiz show team getting beat

2) With everything going quite fine
   They enjoy a nice poem or two that does rhyme
   Before it soon reaches time
   To have something to dine

3) They can then thanks to the sunshine
   Find the sheets dry on the washing line
   And with that also see a sign
   For an evening's restful nice drink of wine

© Paul Wilkins 01/04/2019

A Friend Of Mine

1) When it comes to my friend's Dad
   He's sometimes a little bit sad
   But good jokes from his younger lad
   Make him a lot more glad

2) With my mate's Mum
   She's just occasionally glum
   Though always going up with her thumb
   Once she's had a lot to fill her tum

3) With himself, my mate
   Often getting up a little bit late
   And in the garden sitting on a gate
   Whilst having a little debate

4) This friend and his younger brother
   Also have a good time with each other
   As being brought up nicely by their Father and Mother
   Forever teaching one another

© Paul Wilkins 07/03/2022

A New Promising Friendship

1) Having had a bit of a debate
   I'm willing to with you go on a date
   At quarter past eight
   Until rather late

2) After giving things a think
   We could maybe each have a drink
   Though not having too much or we'd struggle to think
   Which the Police could put down in ink

3) Together being heart to heart
   We could also talk about doing some Art
   A nice drawing club we could start
   With us both playing a part

4) Although I'm not sure when
   It'd also be nice to have a date with you again
   Maybe next Friday at quarter to ten
   In the pub down the road called 'The Hen'

© Paul Wilkins 03/09/2016

A Super Poem about 'Superman'

1) A child on Universal planet Krypton was born
   On a very badly dangerous morn
   Then to avoid suffering death just after his birth
   He was sent by a special space craft to earth

2) After on earth the space craft did land
   A nice farmer and wife took the child in their hand
   To come to terms with things
   They had to come oh quite a length
   When they discovered this child's extremely very big strength

3) This child to be called Clark Kent was in the town Smallville to grow
   With a large number of capabilities to show
   He was a hero called 'Superman' to become
   Who went round saving entirely every-one

4) Superman went to the City of Metropolis to live
   Where at 'The Daily Planet' as Clark Kent
   He had many a news story to give
   With his colleague Lois Lane he became a very good reporter
   Together they did all that they ought ta

5) Clark Kent when changed to 'Superman' solved crime after crime
   Preventing them all including Lex Luthor time after time
   And forever and ever showing he was very brave
   Very many a precious life he did save

© Paul Wilkins 24/02/2012

A True Or Phoney Statement

1) Many a phone call is made today
   Without the slightest bit of delay
   Whether people are with friends or on their own
   They're always busy on their mobile phone

2) After over plenty a different matter
   Members of the public are on their mobile having a chatter
   What they often do next
   Is send one or two people a text

3) Though it's not a very good idea
   People speak on their mobiles just before changing their gear
   Yes whilst travelling quite near and far
   On their phone they chat and chat as they're driving their car

4) One other thing done with mobiles by quite a few
   Is to take a picture of me and you
   Some of which are forever getting dafter
   Though are regularly looked at with lots and lots of laughter

5) Oh well most friends and relations get on well so much
   They should often try and keep in touch
   So even when not face to face together
   You can give each other a call or text whenever

© Paul Wilkins 31/05/2014

AFC Fylde Charity

1) Through AFC Fylde community centre
   First Chris gave me career advice like he was meant ta
   Then to help me all he can
   I had some job hunting tips from Stan
   And for many a good reason
   AFC Fylde Football Club is going up next season

2) Together with their colleagues they're covering oh quite a distance
   To many other people come of assistance
   Along with helping people find a job to do like they ought
   They're encouraging everyone to do a lot more sport
   And for many a good reason
   AFC Fylde Football Club is going up next season

3) Doing everything for a very cheap price
   They're a charity that's quite nice
   Under Supervisor Tom they want to help others out
   And put plenty of effort into that no doubt
   And for many a good reason
   AFC Fylde Football Club is going up next season

4) Working together they also have a G.S.O.H
   And that's not just a rumour
   They have a good team spirit yes
   Which in each business is of value or so I guess
   And for many a good reason
   AFC Fylde Football Club is going up next season

5) We all hope this charity continues to do well
   In what the future has to tell
   Because lots of the Fylde population are going to rely on them
   Time and time again
   And for many a good reason
   AFC Fylde Football Club is going up next season

© Paul Wilkins 24/06/2017

Angels

1) Angels are loving and caring
   Warm heart sharing
   They send plenty of love
   From Lord God above

2) In this world they want happiness and peace
   Never to cease
   But us to have lots of joy
   Not anyone annoy

3) For quite a while
   Angels want us to smile
   Have much happiness and fun
   Whilst getting everything done

4) Angels, from God, are with us forever
   Will desert us never
   But really come of assistance
   In our lives cover oh quite a distance

© Paul Wilkins 19/10/04

Astrological Horoscopes

1) If you are called a Capricorn
   As a very clever person you are born
   Whilst those who are an Aquarius
   Often do things that are quite hilarious

2) When it comes to the Pisces
   They all love sailing the seven seas
   And most of the Aries
   Have a nice big belief in fairies

3) With those who are a Taurus
   Very good at singing in a chorus
   People that are born a Gemini
   Often watch time fly by

4) Each person who is a Cancer
   Is usually a very good dancer
   With a Leo what's most appliant
   Is them each being very reliant

5) Those who are a Virgo
   Have a lot of talent to show
   Each human that's a Libra
   Is always trying to just kid ya

6) With plenty a Scorpio
   Lots of all round good things they do know
   Lastly with people born a Sagittarius
   The food they most enjoy is quite various

© Paul Wilkins 04/08/2013

At The Front Of Blackpool

1) At the end of the pier
   Near the ocean you're getting near
   And you have a good view
   Of there sailing quite a few

2) A good sight you've got
   Of many people on a yacht
   Also many a boat
   All staying afloat

3) To be seen is a nice blue sky
   And I tell no lie
   At the front, in the sun
   A lot of people are having fun

4) Today it's so very hot
   To be inside you should not
   But at the front enjoy a walk
   Whilst having a talk

5) In Blackpool it's been a good day out
   And that's without a doubt
   Now it's time to go back down the pier
   And perhaps go for some beer

© Paul Wilkins 29/07/06

Being Haunted By Ghosts

1) In the house of horrors working as a host
   Quite regularly I have seen many a ghost
   Early in the morning the most
   Just after making myself some toast

2) Together they bring everyone a scare
   They're something to deeply beware
   Moving about here and there
   With us all giving them quite a frightened stare

3) All the ghosts are to be found
   Constantly moving around
   Making a horrible sound
   Sometimes coming from under the ground

4) I hope the Ghostbusters are on their way
   To be here with no delay
   Then we'll say hip hip hurray
   When they've taken all the ghosts away

© Paul Wilkins 26/02/2020

Betting On The Horse Races

1) Whatever your bet
   You will regret
   The horses you choose
   Usually lose

2) It isn't funny
   Often losing money
   Putting too much on a race
   Is a very big disgrace

3) Only when the odds are low
   Can you have a go
   And it often depends on how races begin
   As to whether you will win

4) Some people look at the papers each day
   Pick many a horse without delay
   I don't know how they handle
   Having so much a gamble

© Paul Wilkins 10/04/06

Bugs Bunny

1) One of the cartoon characters who's most funny
   Is the one called Bugs Bunny
   Who whilst looking at many a parrot
   Is very often eating a carrot

2) He's often unable to be found
   Because he's busy underground
   Though he pops up here and there
   Giving every passing thing a stare

3) Sometimes to his big disgrace
   The hunter gives Bugs Bunny a chase
   Though being as good a hider as he ought
   He never ends up being caught

4) Bugs Bunny is always catching the hunter out
   And that's without a doubt
   In the countryside to be found
   He's always running all around

© Paul Wilkins 23/07/2010

Bull's-Eye

1) Me and a friend went to watch some darts competition taking place
Watch our local club's side having another darts club to face
We sat at a pub table with a good view
And got prepared to see what our club's dart side could do

2) On one occasion one of our club's side with the dart hit the bull's-eye of the board
And the crowd came out and applaud
It was an excellent shot with which to win the game
Whilst to the loser it was a shame

3) One of our club's side got treble twenty three times on the trot
Got the highest possible darts score of the lot
He went and retrieved his darts with a smile
He'd not got that maximum score for oh quite a while

4) After a bit the darts competition came to an end
The result was a happy one to me and my friend
Our local club's dart team had gone and had the darts match won
Watching it all had really been fun

© Paul Wilkins 2000

Clever Hercule Poirot

1) The detective Hercule Poirot
   Is a really hero
   He's solved many a crime
   Time after time

2) The first thing he does do
   Is look for a clue
   Searching like many times before
   For who broke the law

3) With the suspicion of quite a few
   He gives many an interview
   Having a very long think
   Whilst also having a drink

4) As handling the investigations
   He makes many observations
   Co-operating with Scotland Yard
   With due regard

5) He then reveals who the Murderer was
   And what this was because
   Explaining what he'd figured out
   And was sure of without a doubt

© Paul Wilkins 20/09/06

Darkness

1) When we go out late at night
   It's not very bright
   The sunshine has gone
   And not as many lights on

2) In the ski, near and far
   There is quite many a star
   Which in the darkness shine
   Over your head and mine

3) When in the darkness I did drive
   The scene wasn't as alive
   There was only a dark view
   Of nice places that I knew

4) At home we all rest in the dark
   Sometimes hearing a dog bark
   And without a bit of light
   Sleep all through the night

© Paul Wilkins 18/04/07

Disability Equality

1) Although it's not always easy to make out
   Lots of people have disabilities without a doubt
   Searching for help without any delay
   They're suffering with difficulties day after day

2) Whilst some people's health problems are obviously on view
   Lots are to be totally unseen too
   As-well as physical there's a lot of mental health problems had
   Which every so often make sufferers a little bit sad

3) At 'Disability Equality North West' we try and come of assistance
   Help people with any health problem cover oh quite a distance
   Time and time again
   We've helped them make a benefit claim

4) To get everything for disabled people going quite fine
   We now run 'Disability Hate Crime'
   So if ever you think you've had some form of discrimination
   Feel free to contact us with no hesitation

5) Although not always up-to lots and lots of employment
   All disabled people should in life have some enjoyment
   So many support charities are being set up in the UK
   Where you can share your problems with no delay

© Paul Wilkins 06/09/2015

European Champions 2022 The England Lionesses

1) The 2022 UEFA European Women's Football Championship has just taken place
   Which was to bring a smile to many an English face
   Because under Manageress Sarina Wiegman they were to get up to their tricks
   And have the biggest triumph, for seniors, since the men in 1966

2) Yes after in the Quarter and Semi final shaking Spain and Sweden up
   In the final they faced Germany, at Wembley, to see who could win the Cup
   In which at the end of normal time there was a draw
   To be followed by extra time once more

3) Then Chloe Kelly scored a deciding goal
   Which at Wembley, attended by 87,192 people, had lots of cheers on the whole
   Also millions of all round TV viewers yes
   Who for the Lionesses victory had lots of celebration or so I guess

4) Prince William then, after medals, presented Captain Leah Williamson with the trophy they'd won
   Whilst having quite a bit of talented fun
   And the Queen praised the Lionesses with deep appreciation
   Calling them 'the inspiration for girls and women today and for the future generation'

5) On a later day England were to have a further EURO 2022 victory celebration at Trafalgar Square
   With about 7000 English fans there
   Looking at an achievement to be given a very big cheer
   And definitely to be mentioned again on BBC 'Sports Personality of The Year'

© Paul Wilkins 01/08/2022

Eye To Eye

1) The colour of your eyes
   You cannot at all disguise
   Because to my one and only heart
   They really play a part
   It definitely seems
   You're the partner of my dreams

2) In them to be seen
   Is the lovely colour green
   And I'm going to look at them
   Time and time again
   It definitely seems
   You're the partner of my dreams

3) If you were to ever go
   A broken heart I'd show
   And giving you a kiss
   I would really miss
   It definitely seems
   You're the partner of my dreams

4) You've forever played a part
   In warming up my heart
   And really showed some care
   Had quite a lot to share
   It definitely seems
   You're the partner of my dreams

5) We're in love, truly so
   Everywhere we go
   Holding hands with a smile
   For oh quite a while
   It definitely seems
   You're the partner of my dreams

© Paul Wilkins 14/09/06

Farming Away

1) The other day at first I didn't twig
   That on my farm there was many a new pig
   Then each of them was having a bit of a dig
   And me, the farmer with cancer, putting on a wig

2) Before much time had gone
   I also saw by the river plenty a swan
   As putting my new coat on
   Which I'd bought without a con

3) Then though not in a rush
   I gave the pavement a quick brush
   Telling a shepherd dog to shush
   Stop distractingly barking near the bush

4) Having put things away in the shed
   I then got ready for bed
   Somewhere to lie down my sweet head
   With the nice wife I one day did wed

© Paul Wilkins 06/08/2021

Getting Up Early In The Morning, Occasionally Yawning

1) It'll soon be time to get the curtains undrawn
   It's now reaching dawn
   Time to stop lying in bed
   Get out and about instead

2) I'll now get up and dressed in my smart clothes
   Before I'm tempted to have another doze
   It'll soon be time to set off to work
   At which if I was late attending I'd look a berk

3) I'll quickly now have some breakfast to digest
   Egg, sausage, bacon and toast together is the best
   Time to see if there's anything in the post
   Nice letters from friends I like the most

4) I'd now better set off to work in my car
   The road looks busy although the distance to travel isn't too far
   That's getting up and together out the way
   Time to see what happens at work and elsewhere through the day

© Paul Wilkins 2000

Going For A Pub Meal

1) We, lunchtime, decided to go out
   And have a good time no doubt
   Never needing to one another shout
   Because none of us are a lazy lout

2) When things are going fine
   They're to be drank to with wine
   Whilst having a dine
   As sat out in the nice sunshine

3) The waitress or waiter will then see if they're able
   To nicely clear our outside based table
   Then in the pub using a cable
   I'll see if to re-power my mobile I'm able

4) We'll then call it a day
   And go on our way
   Without any delay
   Following another busy at the pub Saturday

© Paul Wilkins 09/11/2019

Going To The Library

1) On each and every day
   People go to libraries with no delay
   To after having a careful look
   Choose many an interesting book

2) The various books are then given a date
   That they're to be returned by with no debate
   Or with things not going on time
   The guilty client may face a small fine

3) With the gathering of a few
   Certain clubs meet at the libraries too
   Where they have plenty a table hobby or game event
   Doing just what they're meant

4) The libraries have been going for ages
   Through lots of different life stages
   And are expected to continue for quite a while
   Bringing to members of the public a big smile

© Paul Wilkins 20/01/2024

Healed With All The Power Of Love

1) I once had a very lonely illness
   Bring me to a terrible stillness
   Not at all feeling in top gear
   I was shredding tear after tear
   I'm pleading with the true Lord God above
   I'll soon be healed with all the power of love

2) I'd been in a house of my own
   With no true loving partner to be known
   Although I had plenty of mates out there
   I had no-one offering her warm heart to share
   I'm pleading with the true Lord God above
   I'll soon be healed with all the power of love

3) Thinking, totally wishing like I ought ta
   On the way across the bridge, I threw many a stone in the water
   At each throw that I had a go
   Making many a dream wish for love or so
   I'm pleading with the true Lord God above
   I'll soon be healed with all the power of love

4) Then to a big great surprise
   Some young lady at the other end of the bridge
   Was giving me a sign of love within her eyes
   I gave her a very comforting exchange smile
   Feeling the first sign of happiness I'd had for oh quite a while
   I'm pleading with the true Lord God above
   I'll soon be healed with all the power of love

5) After over the bridge I did walk
   Me, and this lady, had a very heart to heart talk
   Was this at last a friendship or romance on its way
   Helping all my personal problems to all go away
   I'm pleading with the true Lord God above
   I'll soon be healed with all the power of love

© Paul Wilkins 27/07/08

In The British Army

1) In Great Britain we've trained many a soldier
   Most of them each day getting bolder
   Who have to listen to plenty a good coach
   To in war conflicts take the right approach

2) To use different weapons MOD trainees are taught
   So later as qualified soldiers they can do all that they ought
   They're trained to use lots of vehicles too
   Tanks are drove by quite a few

3) In the army you need to be very clever
   With out-witting the enemy your top endeavour
   Each of them also has to be totally quite brave
   For their colleagues and country to save

4) We did well to win the world war
   Having a much bigger challenge than ever before
   And our forces are currently doing all that they can
   Deeply hoping to conclude the battle in Afghanistan

5) Lots of people who've been in the army deserve a medal or two
   Whilst some for deep bravery are given oh quite a few
   Who've each covered really quite a distance
   And to the safety of this and other countries come of great big assistance

© Paul Wilkins 01/07/2012

In The Countryside

1) In the Countryside via sun and rain
   There blossoms many a daisy flower time and time again
   There's also plenty of green grass in the Spring and Summer
   Whilst in the Autumn and Winter it gets much glummer

2) There's many a nice leaved tree too
   Which bird and nest wise attracts quite a few
   Also to them is many a trunk and branch
   Some positioned at a ranch

3) In the Countryside of quite a few
   There's many an animal creature too
   And everywhere different types of birds in the sky
   Flying widely without any kind of a lie

© Paul Wilkins 21/08/2008

Magic Lost But Found

1) There once was a Wizard
   Who got caught in a blizzard
   And he dropped his wand
   Which fell into a pond

2) Getting it back from amongst the fish
   Was now his top wish
   So knowing losing it he'd regret
   He threw in the water a net

3) Soon he managed to regain the wand
   Getting it from a fish that was colour blond
   And he said after losing it was tragic
   Getting it back was magic

4) He then got out his spell book
   At which to have a look
   As a Wizard he then cast one
   Which got the blizzard gone

5) Now the weather was calm
   He felt no harm
   But hoping it would be fine the rest of the day
   He to the castle made his way

© Paul Wilkins 15/06/05

Pets And Owners To The Rescue

1) If ever you have a loneliness regret
   Bring you more company could a pet
   And by being to them kind
   They can deeply relax your mind

2) Most of the time doing like they ought
   Dogs can take you for a regular keep fit walk
   And cats whilst go for a walk on their own
   Would give you nice company when at home

3) Even if to you a dog or cat might take too much time
   Just getting some goldfish could help you feel more fine
   And by taking of your time just a fraction
   From personal, and negative thoughts, they can be distraction

4) So do not be lost at home alone
   When a nice and friendly pet you may own
   And it may take not too much of a distance
   To show each other warm hearted assistance

© Paul Wilkins 06/10/2024

'Ping' Pong Merrily On High

1) Today I will be popping
   To once more do my shopping
   Whilst the prices are still dropping
   Then at home I'll do some mopping

2) After this the trees I will be chopping
   As a friend of mine is very busy copping
   On the beat lots of criminals forever shopping
   Then, with them in court, quite different opinions swapping

© Paul Wilkins 18/07/2021

Poetic Medicine

1) Reading a poem a day
   Keeps your troubles away
   Makes all problems a thing of the past
   Over with at last

2) It's a way of being kind
   Bringing relaxation to your mind
   It's always a joyful humorous time
   Saying many lines that together rhyme

© Paul Wilkins 21/08/2008

Sailing At Sea In The Royal Navy

1) The Royal Navy are forever sailing around the ocean
   Each of the crew after much promotion
   Sometimes by no-one to be seen
   When deep below based in something called a submarine

2) They also sail along in a large boat
   Trying carefully to keep it completely afloat
   If there was a very strong tide
   They couldn't do nothing but hide

3) Many a craft goes across the sea
   Too far out to be seen by you and me
   Lots of different types or so I guess
   Even including an Aircraft Carrier yes

4) The Royal Navy really help our country out
   Make it stay protected from invasion without a doubt
   Being very busy at sea on the whole
   They are always sailing on patrol

5) In some wars they've been very brave
   Had this and other countries to save
   We'll definitely rely on them forever
   And I'm sure them lose their good sea control never

© Paul Wilkins 28/06/2012

Scouting and Abouting

1) It's fun to be a scout
   And that's without a doubt
   You have a real lot to do
   All the year through

2) In a hut each week you meet
   To face another game or feat
   Of badges there is quite a few
   Which can be earned by you

3) In the summer you should make no mistakes
   But go camping in the lakes
   Put up all the tents you require
   And in the evening have a bonfire

4) Going on hikes you can also do
   Or go for a canoe
   Have some enjoyment in the sun
   Together have quite a bit of fun

5) So if in your spare time you get bored
   The idea of joining the scouts is to be applaud
   A chance to get together with many others
   Other than our Fathers and Mothers

© Paul Wilkins 09/05/04

Sharing A Heart

1) All people should give and receive
   All the love in which they believe
   Be loving and caring
   And warm heart sharing
   Everyone wants a partner with whom to play a part
   And really share a heart

2) I often play the guitar in the band
   Using my hand
   And with plenty a love song
   Play my music along
   Everyone wants a partner with whom to play a part
   And really share a heart

3) I'm sure true love is on the way
   Getting nearer day by day
   There'll soon be no more tearfulness
   But you full of cheerfulness
   Everyone wants a partner with whom to play a part
   And really share a heart

4) In this world there's a lot of romance
   Someone with whom to have a lovely dance
   And be together forever
   Alone again never
   Everyone wants a partner with whom to play a part
   And really share a heart

© Paul Wilkins 21/06/05

Sir William Shakespeare

1) William Shakespeare, born in April 1564,
   Became known as 'The English National Poet'
   And now everyone does know it
   He first went to study at Kings New School
   Before as a member of Lord Chamberlain's Men Company of theatrical players
   He proved he was no fool

2) William was brought up with 2 older sisters and 3 younger brothers yes
   Just before he became an all round good writer or so I guess
   Now known by most people including you and me
   He really did lots and lots of poetry

3) William with his writing being extremely very bright
   Became a very good actor and playwright
   Lots and lots of entertainment was to come his way
   Without the slightest bit of delay

4) As now aware of in history by quite a few
   William married Anne Hathaway in November 1582
   Who then mostly had family of their dreams
   Quite sooner than it seems

5) William famously performed time and time again
   Until in 1603 he was even made one of the King's men
   And though he died 400 years ago from today
   His plays and poetry will continue to be read with no delay

© Paul Wilkins 23/04/2016

Sir Winston Churchill

1) Sir Winston Churchill who was to take part in many a war
Was born in Great Britain on 30th November 1874
He went to plenty a different school at a young age
Followed by a studying at Royal Military College stage

2) Churchill had a brief but eventful career in the British Army yes
Getting ready for lots of war involvement or so I guess
Whilst young and in the army doing all that he ought
Churchill regularly wrote a military newspaper report

3) In 1900 Churchill became a Conservative Member of Parliament with no delay
Where he was to have a lot of responsibility at a later day
Soon after this it completely brightened up his life
When Churchill took Clementine Ogilvy Hozier as his special wife

4) On 10th May 1940 King George VI appointed Churchill Prime Minister
And Minister of Defence of the UK
Who needed to go in World War II battle with Adolph Hitler with no delay
Although winning the world war was a very hard deed
With the helpful co-operation of U.S. President Franklin D. Roosevelt
And Soviet Union Leader Joseph Stalin, Churchill and the army did succeed

5) Some-how Churchill faced defeat in the general election in July 1945
Although Knighthood by Queen Elizabeth II in 1953 kept his happiness alive
He then died aged 90 on 24th January 1965 following a severe stroke
Which had him mourned for by lots of British folk

© Paul Wilkins 03/04/2015

Smile And The World Smiles With You

1) Everyone should have a warm heart
   And in having love for one another play a part
   Be very pleasant and polite
   Through each day and night

2) We need to all give each other a grin
   And a very happy life begin
   The more love and joy you give
   The higher with it you do live

3) Happiness is also a key to good health
   Which is worth much more than wealth
   Joy is something wanted by very many
   That doesn't cost a penny

4) Entirely everyone in life does achieve a great lot
   Though think positively of it they do not
   But if you think 'I AM VERY HAPPY' as your endeavour
   Alone, and with others, you'll smile forever

© Paul Wilkins 21/08/04

Some Difficult Poetry

1) In poetry it's frightening
   Each word comes to mind like lightning
   Except a few
   Which are hard to rhyme to

2) Each poet is always having a whinge
   About the word orange
   With which time after time
   You can't find a rhyme

3) Also it's so very rare the word 'objective'
   Because it is so protected
   The word 'happy' is awkward too
   I can't think of a few

4) Oh well I always find a word
   Which is to be heard
   In a poem by me being said
   After me carefully using my bright head

© Paul Wilkins 29/03/06

Someone To Have By My Side In The Countryside

1) I met a friendly lady in the park
   At which my small dog gave a welcome bark
   We gave each other a polite smile and said 'hello'
   Before at having a chat we had a go
   Never let your true dream of love descend
   You'll get the right one in the end

2) At the same time as have an introductive talk
   We through the nice countryside had a short walk
   Observing many a flower and blossomed leaf tree
   A much pleasant atmosphere for her and me
   Never let your true dream of love descend
   You'll get the right one in the end

3) We then having through the forest shared things out
   Had formed a nice friendship without a doubt
   We to have a rest, on the countryside bench took a seat
   To chat a little bit more, whilst resting each of our feet
   Never let your true dream of love descend
   You'll get the right one in the end

4) Then whilst I noticed a nice leaf fall from a tree
   She said she'd like to keep in touch with me
   We gave each other a contact note without a lie
   Before I gave her a pleasant kiss goodbye
   Never let your true dream of love descend
   You'll get the right one in the end

© Paul Wilkins 27/07/08

Take A Break By Playing Snooker

1) Pot black was the first snooker programme on T.V.
To be enjoyably watched by you and me
All the players got busy with their cue
For them to fully entertain quite a few
The snooker players are always busy with their cue and chalk
As round the table having a brisk walk

2) Then with the popularity of snooker going fine
Lots of competition was shown on BBC T.V.
introduced by David Vine
Showing how good everyone was with their snooker cue
By Clive Everton and John Virgo live commentary was given too
The snooker players are always busy with their cue and chalk
As round the table having a brisk walk

3) Steve Davis, Cliff Thorburn and 1 or 2 others took their time
Intending each snooker shot to go absolutely fine
Whilst players like Jimmy White and later Ronnie O'Sullivan made all the live spectators shush
When they played each of their shots in a mad rush
The snooker players are always busy with their cue and chalk
As round the table having a brisk walk

4) In the game of snooker to get to the max
You need to successfully pot 15 reds and 15 blacks
Then you require to pot the yellow to black
Or if miss just one colour bring your maximum break a big sack
The snooker players are always busy with their cue and chalk
As round the table having a brisk walk

5) As at snooker many players are having quite much fun
There's also plenty a Professional Trophy to be won
Some players like Steve Davis and Stephen Hendry
have been constant winners
Whilst on the whole there's also good beginners
The snooker players are always busy with their cue and chalk
As round the table having a brisk walk

© Paul Wilkins 13/04/2012

The 1966 FIFA World Cup

1) In the 1966 UK hosted FIFA World Cup
England went on to shake all the others up
Under Manager Alf Ramsey they won game after game
Which to all the others was quite a shame

2) In the quarter-finals England beat Argentina 1-0
Including a goal from Geoff Hurst which was quite a thrill
Whilst in the semi-finals England beat Portugal 2-1
With Bobby Charlton scoring twice and Portugal having a successful penalty,
Just before the final whistle was gone

3) Then in a very close final England had Germany to face
Which following a 2-2 draw it meant extra time needed to take place
Geoff Hurst then with 2 more goals, 1 questionable, took England 4-2 up
So when the whistle finally went, at London Wembley Stadium,
They could deeply celebrate winning the 'World Cup'

4) With lots and lots of all round rejoicing to be seen
The England players each received a 'Gold Medal', and team winning 'Trophy',
From the completely delighted Queen
Bringing to everyone in England a smile
This was published and mentioned everywhere for oh quite a while

5) Having taken the England football team to Heaven
The Manager Alf Ramsey even got given 'Knighthood' in January 1967
This football achievement will be one to deeply remember and treasure
And go down as a terrific England historic event forever and ever

© Paul Wilkins 11/10/2017

The Best Of Preston City

1) In Preston City a lot takes place
   To bring a smile to many a face
   People are forever here popping
   To do lots and lots of shopping

2) A large number of students come lodging here too
   Because 'The University of Central Lancashire' is attended by oh quite a few
   Without the slightest bit of hesitation
   For all these students there's regularly being built more and more accommodation

3) Plenty of sport takes place in Preston also yes
   The Guild Hall is often well attended or so I guess
   Because lots of entertainment, including Professional Snooker, takes place there
   Bringing deeply interested spectators from completely everywhere

4) Also at Preston Deepdale football ground
   'PNE Football Club' are quite often to be found
   Who each weekend have many a supporter
   All cheering them on to 'Win' like they ought ta

5) Every twenty years a Preston City 'Guild Year' brings a smile to all local peoples face
   Which involves lots of entertainment, including street processions taking place
   So we all hope everyone when in Preston has a good time
   And everything planned goes quite extremely fine

© Paul Wilkins 23/10/2007

The Cowboys

1) There used to be many a cowboy in the west
   Facing a big test
   On the saddle of their horses
   They galloped very long courses

2) With duties together shared
   They handled plenty a herd
   Keeping them together
   Whilst travelling forever

3) Occasionally without any fun
   They all had to use their gun
   Such as when Indians caused a raid
   And made all the cattle afraid

4) Also with a bit of fright
   In some towns there was a gunfight
   Seeing like other times before
   Who was quickest on the draw

5) Sheriffs were also once called for
   When there was many an outlaw
   There really was a lot of western battle in the past
   Though it's now over with at last

© Paul Wilkins 23/08/06

The Dangerous Fire Of Smoke

1) When I say 'I saw a building of smoke'
   It was not at all a joke
   Without me being anything like a liar
   There was in-front of me a very big fire

2) Whilst I had a lot of safety to learn
   Each part of my house continued to burn
   I was beginning to say 'Flipping heck'
   Noticing my home become a wreck

3) Although now another home I would require
   Thank goodness no-one was hurt in the fire
   The firemen gradually putting it out
   And doing that well without a doubt

4) As passers-by needed to beware
   Smoke was spreading everywhere
   It was soon to be all put out though
   And me in life to have another go

© Paul Wilkins 13/01/10

The Heroes Batman and Robin

1) Bruce Wayne through having his parents killed at a young age
   Was to grow up into a crime fighting stage
   Becoming Batman he wanted evil a thing of the past
   Completely over with at last

2) Batman and soon to be found friend Robin did what they could
   To have crime in Gotham City as rare as it should
   Because yes without a single doubt
   They were here to help the Police out

3) Don't ask me at all why
   But the Cat-woman was pretty sly
   Also the Penguin is said to be a wicked fella
   Always getting up to mischief while carrying his umbrella

4) The caped crusaders had to get to unlawful incidents in a dash
   Whilst in the bat-mobile trying to avoid having a crash
   When it comes to the Joker
   As laughing he's always cheating at poker

5) Without Batman and Robin we'd be in trouble yes
   They're heroes of this City or so I guess
   Keeping everything safe on many a street
   Getting in Prison all the different criminals who are facing defeat

© Paul Wilkins 08/02/2014

The Life Of Dame Agatha Christie

1) Agatha Christie was born on the 15th September 1890 in Torquay
   Later to be seen as a star writer by you and me
   She was to go on to publish 66 detective novels yes
   And a 14 short story collection or so I guess

2) Agatha trained as a travel nurse during the 1st World War
   Before becoming the most popular novelists ever seen before
   With her first publication a century ago
   In 1920 being 'The Mysterious Affair at Styles' involving Hercule Poirot

3) Agatha married Archibold Christie 1914 until 1928
   Though after having one child called Rosalind Hicks they divorced at a later date
   In 1930 until 1976 she was to marry archaeologist Max Mallowan though
   And as-well as tour with him she'd have a lot more books to everyone show

4) Agatha was to publish plenty a Hercule Poirot and Miss Marple story for you and me
   At a later date to be seen as detective stories on TV
   Her play 'The Mousetrap' was shown at the London theatre in 1952
   Which has been performed again and again, with no break, to be seen by oh quite a few

5) In regard of everything she had done
   Agatha was appointed 'Dame Commander Of The British Empire' in 1971
   Then on the 12th January 1976 in Winterbrook sadly she did die
   Though all her different stories will remain popular worldwide without a single lie

© Paul Wilkins 20/12/2020

The Life Of Martin Luther King

1) Martin Luther King was born in Atlanta, Georgia, United States on the 15th January 1929
   And his career was to go quite fine
   Becoming an American Baptist Minister yes
   Who was to lots of different people bless

2) Martin was married to Coretta Scott 1953 to 1968
   Having 4 nice children following a little debate
   Then he became Prominent Leader in civil rights movement
   Leading protest marches after a big improvement

3) Martin led action against Jim Crow Laws and other forces of discrimination
   Doing so with not a bit of hesitation
   Combating racial inequality through non-violent resistance too
   Which had him proud of an October 1964 'Nobel Peace Prize' for helping out quite a few

4) Then Martin was Assassinated on the 4th April 1968
   With lots of loss felt with no debate
   And national mourning soon took place
   With plenty a very sad looking face

5) Whilst in the United States staying around
   The rights of many others Martin had really successfully found
   Awarded 'Presidential Medal Of Freedom' in 1977
   Followed in 2003 by a 'Congressional Gold Medal' for him in Heaven

© Paul Wilkins 31/10/2022

The Manchester United 2007/08 Double

1) Through 'Sir Alex Ferguson', Man United got the double again this year
   Something for all us Man U supporters to drink to with beer
   Although towards the Premiership end Chelsea put some pressure on
   Our hopes of winning were still not at all gone

2) Through 'Christiano Ronaldo' scoring so many a goal
   He was the season's best player as a whole
   'Giggs' was to pick up his 10th Premiership season win
   Which brought to his face a very special grin

3) Having beat Chelsea in the 2007/08 Premiership yes
   Who were Man United to face in the European Championship, have a guess
   It was to be a very close action game, including extra time, no doubt
   Which led to a concluding very tense penalty shoot-out

4) There was first tension when 'Ronaldo' missed his penalty kick
   With keeper 'Petr Cech' with his save doing the trick
   But 'Edwin Van Der Sar', in goal, was by stopping 'John Terry'
   And 'Nicolas Anelka' do even better
   Making Chelsea Manager 'Avram Grant' once more a big regretter

5) Yes the Old Trafford Manager of a very special kind
   Was to a second European Championship Trophy for his team find
   'Sir Alex Ferguson' and his tremendous Man United team
   Were celebrating with the fans, for ages, such a come true dream

© Paul Wilkins 31/07/08

The Royal Air Force (RAF)

1) The RAF can be seen flying many an aeroplane
   Extremely time and time again
   And I'm not telling a lie
   When I say they go all over the sky

2) The spitfire came to the rescue in the war
   Winning a battle in the air never seen before
   It really was a well flown ideal plane
   That had Hitler and all of Germany giving up in sane

3) There's a lot of pilots in the RAF
   Some who sadly in wars have suffered death
   But mostly ones who've gone on to succeed
   Whatever their high flying challenging deed

4) The RAF need to speed their planes down the runway
   To take off with no at all delay
   And then they have a very good view
   Whilst flying highly above me and you

5) Over the years there's been plenty an air show
   With supreme pilots at real high-up stunts having a go
   Often in the sky on show all of the red arrows
   At the same time as scaring off some of the nice sparrows

© Paul Wilkins 29/06/2012

The School Crossing Patrol Officers

1) The lollipop man and lady have lots of regard
   Working on the road near the school yard
   Bringing all the traffic to a slow stop
   To let all the children over the road pop

2) They work mostly early morning and mid afternoon
   When children are going to start or finish school soon
   Covering oh quite a distance
   Throughout the UK coming of great big assistance

3) The lollipop man and lady need to be brave
   To lots of lives carefully save
   Being very extremely bold yes
   Keeping crossing the roadway from getting in a mess

4) Together many an accident they prevent
   Getting drivers and pedestrians doing just what they're meant
   Making sure everyone is safe instead of sorry
   By slowing down plenty a dangerous car and lorry

© Paul Wilkins 17/04/2024

The Staircase

1) With many a different staircase you can go up and down
   Showing on your face a smile or a frown
   And whilst trying to never decline
   You can take everything one step at a time

2) Having made it all the way to the top
   To gain your breath you need to for a moment stop
   Then on the very top floor
   You can give each room a vacuum clean once more

3) At the top of your building you also have a good view
   And of your neighbours can see oh quite a few
   They're all to be seen near and far
   Busy in the garden or cleaning their car

4) When going down seeing to floor after floor
   You get tired once more
   But if in your house you don't want a mouse or lots of dust
   Clean it all quite regularly you really must

5) Once all the total cleaning is complete
   In the living room, on the ground floor, you can put up your feet
   And having workwise been put to a big test
   Whilst having a brew, and watching TV, you can at last have a rest

© Paul Wilkins 20/08/2017

The Temptation Of Chocolate

1) It's just gone past a nice Christmas time
   When everything's been going fine
   Except with some regard for my weight
   Which has been getting a little bit heavier, without debate
   I'm always suffering temptation
   Eating chocolate with no hesitation

2) About chocolate cakes and sweets please be a little bit quiet
   Because I think I deeply require to go on a diet
   It'll be necessary for me to be careful in which shops I go
   Not wanting to see too many chocolates out on show
   I'm always suffering temptation
   Eating chocolate with no hesitation

3) A couple of months have now gone by
   And I've got a little more thinner, no lie
   But now Easter's getting nearer day by day
   With Easter eggs soon possibly coming my way
   I'm always suffering temptation
   Eating chocolate with no hesitation

4) There's one area in which chocolate plays a special part
   Which is in keeping healthier many a heart
   Yes as-well as naughty, it can be good
   When eaten in small quantities, as you should
   I'm always suffering temptation
   Eating chocolate with no hesitation

© Paul Wilkins 1996

The World Hero Nelson Mandela

1) Nelson Mandela was born in South Africa in 1918 yes
   In it was to bring quite a big change or so I guess
   Taking action against it with no hesitation
   He was imprisoned for 27 years
   For his opposition of Government Racial Discrimination

2) Following many a fairness in his Country's plea
   Nelson was in 1990 to everyone's joy set free
   Managing to unite the disparate warring parties
   And avoid South Africa civil war
   In 1993 he was awarded the Nobel Peace Prize
   And was to feel better than ever before

3) In 1994 Nelson was made the first Black President of South Africa yes
   Something to be deeply celebrated or so I guess
   To now start a much more happy life
   In 1998 he took Graca Machel as his true wife

4) Nelson was to empower disadvantaged children
   And fight against HIV/Aids as much as he could
   Getting everyone in South Africa living as fairly as they should
   Having brought together more peace and happiness than ever before
   He retired from being a great President in the year 2004

5) Although he'd got lots of things in this world to go to perfection
   Starting in 2011 Nelson was sadly to suffer lung infection
   In December 2013 he was to many people's upset die
   Though world-wide he'll be remembered as a hero without a lie

© Paul Wilkins 07/03/2014

Together Keeping Afloat

1) Whilst wearing a nice and warm coat
   I once went out on a boat
   Which was quite well keeping afloat
   As I had a brew for my bad throat

2) To be seen on a near island was a goat
   That appeared to eating some oat
   About which with interest we all wrote
   Without any form of gloat

3) On this trip everyone made many a note
   Making the different sentences together float
   For the best writer there to be a vote
   And the overall prize winner someone quote

4) The touring winning writer was Mr Yoat
   Who had totally a large amount wrote
   Including a bit about the goat
   That when passing by lots of people did note

© Paul Wilkins 14/02/2024

Tom And Jerry

1) There was a cat in the house
   Who was always after a mouse
   Whenever it was by the cat found
   It chased it all round

2) The mouse that was mostly merry
   Was nicely called Jerry
   Whilst the cat, who was a naughty one
   Was one called Tom

3) Wanting to eat him with a cherry
   Tom was always after Jerry
   With many a trip and fall to be found
   He pursued him all around

4) One day Tom scared Jerry in the garden
   Where the dog said 'I beg your pardon'
   'But Jerry is my friend'
   'Bring your chasing him to an end'

5) Looking at the angry dog, Tom did obey
   And went back in the house with no delay
   Leaving the dog keeping protected and safe Jerry
   Who now again felt very merry

© Paul Wilkins 10/08/06

Treble Win In Season 1998/99

1) In the football season 1998/99
   For Sir Alex Ferguson and Manchester United everything went fine
   At the end of it they made all the front pages
   Being the first treble winners for absolutely ages

2) Managing to not too many points drop
   In the Premiership League they finished top
   Then with a penalty save from Peter Schmeichel won the FA Cup
   By really being able to in the final shake Newcastle United up

3) In the European Championship for Bayern Munich 1-0 up
   Everything was going fine
   Because it had now gone completely into stoppage time
   Then suddenly Teddy Sherringham with a good shot disguiser
   Tremendously for Man United got a superb equaliser

4) Next still in stoppage time came a shock on the whole
   When substitute Ole Gunnar Solskjaer got a brilliant game winning goal
   Soon holding it up for all the fans to see
   They were celebrating winning the Cup quite definitely

5) David Beckham, Jaap Stam, Dwight Yorke, and Andy Cole
   And all the rest of the team
   Had this season made come true Sir Alex's dream
   Who getting each Man United player doing all that they should
   Went on to also be given a great rewarding 'Knighthood'

© Paul Wilkins 16/06/2012

Ukraine Today

1) When it comes to Ukraine
   Now shipped from it other countries can hopefully have grain
   To ease their food shortage pain
   Which they've gone through time and again

2) Reliant on a Russia deal
   Lots of foreigners could have a much bigger meal
   And once again at ease feel
   With some better thought becoming real

3) Next we want the war to reach an end
   The number of people suffering to deeply descend
   Ukraine and Russia to once more be-friend
   And bring to this world a big mend

4) So please let weapons be put away
   And in war there be less of a frown today
   But peace and happiness once more on it's way
   With not much delay

© Paul Wilkins 22/07/2022

Vice-Admiral Horatio Nelson

1) Admiral Nelson was born in Burnham Thorpe on the 29th September 1758
   He did well at Kind Edward VI's Grammar School with no debate
   His naval career then began via his Uncle in January 1771
   And as a British flag officer he developed before much time had gone

2) Admiral Nelson was to take part in many a British naval victory yes
   Mostly through Napoleonic wars or so I guess
   Though in battle at Corsica at age 35 he lost sight of one eye
   And use of one arm when he was 40 no lie

3) To bring him and lots of others more of a smile
   There was victory over the French with Battle of the Nile
   Admiral Nelson was to pick up plenty a medal and statue award
   Including 'Knight of the Order of the Bath' for which he was deeply applaud

4) Frances Herbert Woolward, Admiral Nelson was to marry in 1787
   Although Lady Emma Hamilton was also to take him to heaven
   But to bring them both some bad pain
   On the 21st October 1805 he was to die in the Battle of Trafalgar, in Spain

5) The Battle of Trafalgar was to be the greatest victory, though
   Admiral Nelson having his Quote 'Thank God I have done my duty' as his last words to
   show
   And he was buried on the 9th January 1806 in St Paul's Cathedral in the City of London
   With many a broken British heart by him won

© Paul Wilkins 28/12/2020

What 'We' Did Together

1) We had promotion
   We sailed the ocean
   We showed lots of devotion
   We shared plenty of emotion

2) We were then at the land
   We played in the sand
   We gave each other a hand
   We tried not to deeply demand

3) We then went for a meal
   We wanted a fair deal
   We were after something quite real
   We wanted to give our hunger a heal

4) We conclusively went home
   We were then each on our own
   We had lots of friendship earlier shown
   We were never too long alone

© Paul Wilkins 22/11/2023

William Wordsworth

1) William Wordsworth was born on the 7th April 1770 yes
   And that was in Cockermouth, Cumberland, or so I guess
   He was then brought up at Hawkeshead Grammar School
   Where with his English he was no fool

2) Wordsworth went to St John's College too
   Also at the University of Oxford, and Cambridge, joined quite a few
   And he was to become an English Romantic poet
   With lots of different people to soon get to know it

3) In 1793 Wordsworth had his first poetry publication
   Which proved popular with no hesitation
   Then following a little bit of debate
   He published 'Lyrical Ballads' in 1798

4) In 1802 Wordsworth took Mary Hutchinson as his wife
   Who, with 5 children, managed to liven up his life
   And they each quite definitely
   Enjoyed listening to his all round poetry

5) Wordsworth then became Poet Laureate in 1843
   Doing lots of writing still to be seen by you and me
   With him continuing so for a total of 7 successive years
   Until his death on the 23rd April 1850 brought some tears

© Paul Wilkins 14/11/2021

Worldwide Climate Change

1) When it comes to the worldwide climate change
   Much more intense drought, storms and heat waves are quite a high range
   Rising sea levels, melting glaciers and warming oceans also bringing to animals harm
   Including on many a different farm

2) To rid of this climate change frown
   On coal, oil and gas we need to cut down
   Or if entirely all countries do not
   It'll soon be everywhere getting much too hot

3) Climate change affects the social and environmental determinants of health
   Which are much more important than wealth
   If we don't worldwide quickly take action
   The number of people and animals suffering will increase by a very big fraction

4) So, to bring the temperature down
   We need to all stop using coal, oil and gas like a clown
   But everywhere start having a careful thought
   And be using things like electricity more as we ought

© Paul Wilkins 19/07/2022

www.ingramcontent.com/pod-product-compliance
Lightning Source LLC
Chambersburg PA
CBHW070327120526
44590CB00017B/2828